Anglo-Saxons for Kids

A Captivating Guide to the People of Early Medieval England and Their Battles Against the Vikings

Table of Contents

INTRODUCTION

Have you ever wondered if King Arthur was real? Have you ever wondered where the English language came from and why it can be so strange? Have you ever wondered who came after the Romans left Britain? Look no further than the Anglo-Saxons! The Anglo-Saxons were tribes who came to Britain from Northern Germany in the fifth century. They conquered the people living there and made Britain their own country.

The Anglo-Saxons did more than just take over Britain. They were also very important in setting up the political, religious, and social structure of England. We still use these structures today! Before the Anglo-Saxons arrived, Britain had several warring tribes. The Anglo-Saxons created kingdoms. At first, there were many kingdoms, but eventually, they all became one. This created the English monarchy.

The Anglo-Saxons ruled Britain when missionaries first arrived with Christianity. The missionaries converted the Anglo-Saxons, who established church structures. They even created powerful positions like the Archbishop of Canterbury! These church structures didn't just change the religious world in Britain but all places where people practiced Christianity.

The Anglo-Saxons aren't ruling England anymore, but their impact can still be felt over one thousand years later. Both students and parents will enjoy reading this fun, up-to-date history of these important historic people. This book has everything you need to learn about the people, places, and ideas that made the Anglo-Saxons so important to world history. Get ready to set sail for a time filled with rival kings, intricate jewelry, and Vikings. The Anglo-Saxon time in British history changed the course of the world one king at a time.

Chapter 1: What's an Anglo-Saxon?

The history of England is filled with people coming and going. Even the Roman Empire spent some time in England! The Romans built roads and cities, but they didn't stay forever. After the Romans left, the people in Britain thought they could go back to their lives, but they were wrong. As soon as the Romans left, a new group of people from Europe invaded. They were called the **Anglo-Saxons**. They also set up their own villages and divided England into different kingdoms. Many of these old divisions are still used today!

But who were the Anglo-Saxons? They were the people who ruled England between the time of the Romans and the **Norman Conquest**. That's over 500 years! These people were powerful and helped make Britain the country it is today.

But did you know that the Anglo-Saxons didn't call themselves that? The term "Anglo-Saxon" was first used in the late eighth century, many years after the Anglo-Saxons had invaded. People in Europe needed a way to distinguish between the Saxons living in Europe and those living in Britain.

The Saxons were only one of the groups that came to Britain. There were three major groups of people who invaded and settled in England. They were the **Angles**, the **Saxons**, and the **Jutes**. When they settled in England, they became the one group we know as the Anglo-Saxons.

These three groups came from the same area: ancient Germany. They were **Germanic tribes**, and they farmed near the **North Sea**. They were good warriors, and they also did a lot of sailing.

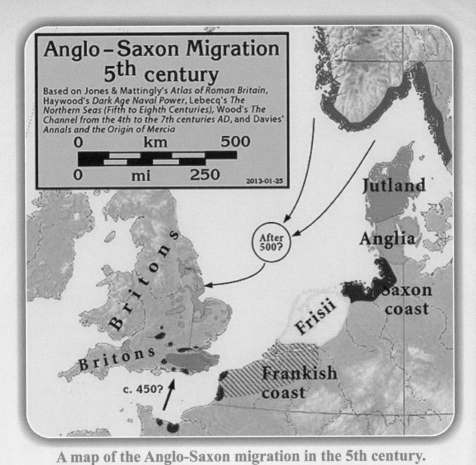

A map of the Anglo-Saxon migration in the 5th century.

But why did the Anglo-Saxons come to Britain? Historians disagre
about why the Anglo-Saxons first traveled to England. Some thin
they were looking for good farmland. Others think that the Anglo-
Saxons were invited by **Vortigern**. At this time, the people living
England were called **Britons**, but they weren't the only people livin
there. There were also people in modern-day Scotland called th
Picts and the **Scotti**. These groups fought a lot, and in the fift
century, Vortigern was a Briton ruler. He knew the Anglo-Saxon
were good warriors, so some historians believe he asked them
come to help him fight the Scotti and the Picts. This may hav

accidentally started the Anglo-Saxon invasion. Can you imagine how Vortigern must have felt? He wanted help defending his country, and the people he asked to help began invading it themselves!

A depiction of the Anglo-Saxons crossing the ocean.

The Anglo-Saxons didn't take over Britain all at once. You might think invasions are fast, but the Anglo-Saxon invasion took centuries. They started on the east coast of Britain and slowly pushed west. The Britons didn't like the Anglo-Saxons, and there was a lot of fighting. Still, the Anglo-Saxons slowly moved across the country, pushing the other people west into **Wales** or north into **Scotland**. They also set up **kingdoms** as they went. As more Anglo-Saxons moved to Britain, the kingdoms began fighting against each other as well. Remember, the Anglo-Saxons were actually three different groups. These groups didn't always work together, which is why the Anglo-Saxon kingdoms fought with each other for land, power, and resources.

One reason we know so much about the Anglo-Saxons is that an English historian wrote about them. His name was the **Venerable Bede**, and he lived from about 674 to 735 CE. Historians think he was born in Monkton, Durham, but we don't know anything about his childhood until he was seven. At seven years old, he was placed in the monastery of St. Peter's at Wearmouth. He later moved to the monastery at **Jarrow**, where he lived the rest of his life.

Living in the monastery, the Venerable Bede was surrounded by books. When he wasn't focused on his religious duties as a priest, he spent much time reading and writing. He wrote about 40 books in his life. Many of them deal with religious topics, but the Venerable Bede also liked history.

The Venerable Bede wrote all about English history in his book *The Ecclesiastical History of the English People*. Many historians today think of the Venerable Bede as the **Father of English History**. If you were the Venerable Bede, what kinds of events would you include in your history book?

The Venerable Bede wanted to tell the story of Christianity in Britain. His book starts with the arrival of **Saint Augustine** in Britain and talks about how he helped convert the Anglo-Saxons to Christianity. The book also contains stories about how the Anglo-Saxons arrived in Britain and their history. His book has been very important in helping historians learn about the Anglo-Saxons in Britain.

The Anglo-Saxons needed time to work through all the tumult, but eventually, they settled down. They started farms and set up local kings. The Anglo-Saxons helped set up the different **political areas** in Britain today. At first, each of these areas was a little kingdom. Although the Anglo-Saxon kingdoms were similar, each kingdom had its own culture and laws. Even though England eventually united under one king, the boundaries of these different kingdoms stayed. These ancient boundaries are still in place today! The people also preserved some of the culture of their **shires**, which continues to be a treasured part of modern British culture.

Even though the Anglo-Saxons were important to British history, they did not rule forever. In 1066, the Anglo-Saxons fell from power during the **Norman Conquest**. Most of the Anglo-Saxon nobility fled or lost their power. The Normans set up their own kings and nobility. Even though they were no longer kings, the Anglo-Saxons continued to write their stories and live their lives just as they did before, continuing to shape England into the country it is today.

Chapter 1 Challenge Activity

Can you solve this word search puzzle?

B	B	P	S	R	L	V	O	A	E	I	E	A	N
I	G	R	O	N	O	R	T	H	S	E	A	N	O
M	N	G	A	B	O	A	T	S	N	N	I	V	R
O	I	N	A	N	B	E	D	E	A	I	D	G	M
R	M	M	S	M	I	K	A	U	O	T	O	O	A
G	R	S	E	C	V	N	I	J	U	T	E	S	N
N	A	T	L	S	O	R	F	N	T	B	M	D	N
O	F	R	G	B	R	O	S	M	G	K	M	E	P
X	G	E	N	R	T	M	J	A	M	D	V	R	S
A	S	N	A	I	I	A	N	B	M	T	O	A	M
S	L	F	N	T	G	N	N	N	T	A	G	M	A
I	A	N	A	O	E	B	P	I	C	T	S	R	S
I	T	I	N	N	R	T	F	F	N	N	T	A	B
E	M	E	N	C	N	F	I	T	B	N	A	O	C

ROMAN
JUTES
VORTIGERN
ANGLES
KINGDOMS
NORTH SEA
BRITON
SAXON
BOATS
BEDE
PICTS
FARMING
NORMAN

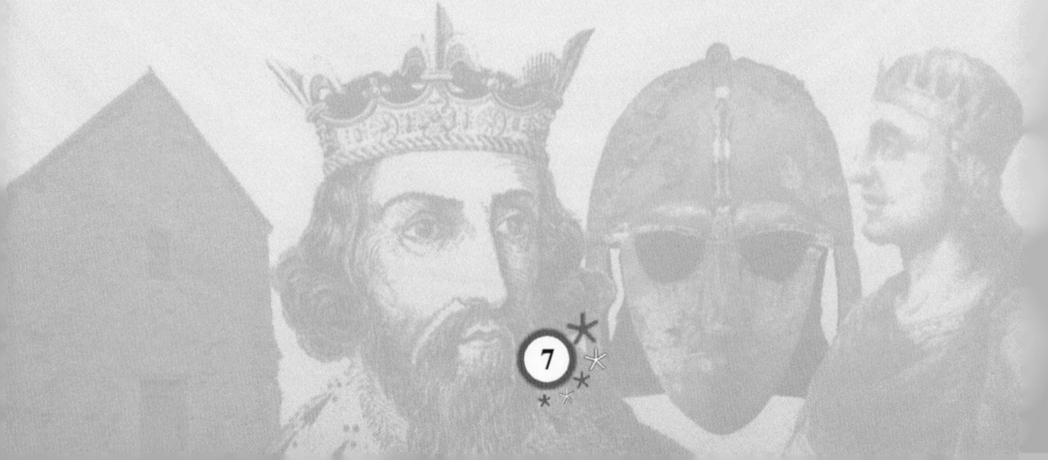

Chapter 2: Kingdoms of Anglo-Saxon Britain

Anglo-Saxon Britain was not one united country. The people didn't all listen to one ruler or even follow the same laws! Instead, Anglo-Saxon Britain was divided into a lot of different **kingdoms**. Each kingdom acted like its own country. They **allied** with each other, and they fought against each other. Much of Anglo-Saxon history is filled with stories of the different kingdoms fighting against each other. Sometimes, they even took each other over!

Even though there were many different kingdoms in Britain, there were seven main kingdoms with similar governments. Each kingdom was started by a group of Anglo-Saxons led by a **war chief**. Eventually, the war chief became powerful enough that he became a **king**. The king was in charge of the army. That means there were at least seven little armies in Britain during parts of the Anglo-Saxon time! Can you imagine how much fighting there must have been with seven armies?

Even though there was chaos during parts of Anglo-Saxon history, the people were not lawless. There were rules and laws everyone in the kingdom had to follow. And the punishments for breaking the laws were severe. There weren't any prisons, so if you broke the law, you might have to pay a fine, or you might be executed. They even had a special fine called **wergild** (where-gild). It literally means "man price." If someone killed someone else, they had to pay a lot of money to their family. A wergild was the price of the life that was taken. The Anglo-Saxons had this special fine to prevent revenge and **blood feuds**. A blood feud is when two families fight each other for a very long time, sometimes even for generations! Many people died in blood feuds, and the Anglo-Saxons didn't want more chaos in their kingdoms. Paying a fine to stop revenge might seem strange to us, but the Anglo-Saxon laws helped the kings keep order in their kingdoms.

As the kingdoms fought with each other, they changed over time. Many of the kingdoms started out small. As the Anglo-Saxons pushed west, they took over more land that had belonged to the Britons, making their kingdoms bigger.

The Anglo-Saxons settlements in the early 7th century.
Hel-hama, CC BY-SA 3.0 <http://creativecommons.org/licenses/by-sa/3.0/>,
via Wikimedia Commons; https://commons.wikimedia.org/wiki/File:England_878.svg

One of the most important kingdoms early in Anglo-Saxon history was **Northumbria**. It was in the northern part of Anglo-Saxon Britain and was originally settled by the Angles. Northumbria was formed from two separate states called **Bernicia** (ber-knee-sea-uh) and **Deira** (day-ruh). The two states came together under **King Æthelfrith** (ethel-frith), and the kingdom continued to expand north whenever possible. Northumbria was most powerful during the seventh century. It has a strong army and several powerful monasteries. We might not think of monasteries as powerful places today, but back in Anglo-Saxon times, they were centers of learning. In the eighth century, Northumbria fell in importance because many people were fighting to be king. The inner chaos made it hard for Northumbria to remain strong against the other Anglo-Saxon kingdoms.

Directly south of Northumbria was **Mercia**. This kingdom was in the middle of Britain. This made the kingdom hard to defend because it was surrounded by other kingdoms. Much of Mercia's history is filled with battles to keep its boundaries safe and protect its people. During the seventh century and eighth centuries, Mercia was strong enough to defend itself and even expand its territory. The most famous Mercian king was **King Offa**. He ruled for 39 years and had power over other kingdoms like Wessex and East Anglia. He is most famous for constructing **Offa's Dyke**. This wall ran between Wales and Mercia, and you can still see parts of it today. However, after King Offa died, Mercia fell in importance and lost its ability to rule itself by the tenth century.

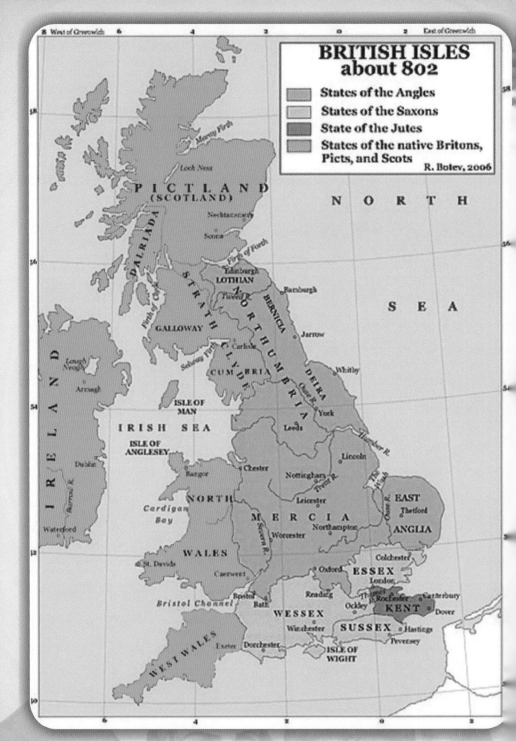

BRITISH ISLES about 802

States of the Angles
States of the Saxons
State of the Jutes
States of the native Britons, Picts, and Scots

R. Botev, 2006

Britain in the early 9th century.
https://commons.wikimedia.org/wiki/File:Britain_802.jpg

To the east of Mercia, on the eastern edge of Britain, was the kingdom called **East Anglia**. East Anglia was founded by both Angles and Saxons. Historians believe East Anglia began around 571 CE. The people in East Anglia were very good at making boats. They used the rivers in East Anglia to sail farther into Britain and even used boats to bury important people. The most famous burial boat is called **Sutton Hoo**. Historians believe this burial was for **King Rædwald** (reed-wald). The king's body was placed on board along with things he would need in the next life, including armor and weapons. Can you imagine being buried on a boat? Historians have learned a lot about the Anglo-Saxons by studying the Sutton Hoo burial.

East Anglia was ruled by Mercia for some time but won back its independence in the ninth century.

South of Mercia was the kingdom of **Wessex.** Wessex is one of the most famous Anglo-Saxon kingdoms because it was able to fight against the Vikings for so long. The name "Wessex" comes from "West Saxon." The kingdom was founded early in Anglo-Saxon history, but it did not come to prominence until the ninth century. Before that, the kings of Wessex were busy fighting with the Britons in modern-day Wales, Mercia, and Northumbria. When Mercia fell, Wessex expanded and began growing stronger. When the Vikings arrived, Wessex was strong enough to stand against them. The most famous Wessex king was **King Alfred the Great**, who became the king of all of England that was not under Viking rule. This was an important step towards uniting the country.

These were the four main kingdoms in Anglo-Saxon Britain, but three other minor kingdoms were also important during this period.

Sussex was located on the southern coast of Britain, south of London and east of Wessex. Sussex was founded around 477 CE. The kingdom was not independent for long. By the 800s, Sussex had been conquered by Wessex. Sussex was a poor kingdom, especially compared to the other Anglo-Saxon kingdoms. The people's clothes and metalwork were plainer, suggesting they didn't have much money. However, they spent the money they had on fancy food and impressive architecture.

Kent was east of Sussex, and it was the earliest Anglo-Saxon kingdom. Kent was founded around 455 CE by the Jutes. Some stories say that Kent was founded by the Jutes whom King Vortigern invited to Britain to help him fight the Picts, but historians are not certain. However the Jutes arrived, they lived with the Britons who were already there. The Jutes weren't strong enough to drive the Britons out completely. Kent continued as a minor kingdom in the southeast of Britain until it became part of Wessex around 860 CE.

Essex was located between Kent and East Anglia. Essex was founded around 500 CE by the Saxons. Essex worked very closely with Kent but the Essex government sometimes divided its kingdom into multiple territories. That means Essex sometimes had several kings at once. This was a little different than how the bigger kingdoms ran their governments. Even though Essex had London, it was never a big kingdom and was given to the Vikings during the ninth century.

Chapter 2 Challenge Activity

Can you label the seven main kingdoms of Anglo-Saxon Britain on the map below?

Kent   Northumbria   East Anglia   Sussex

Wessex   Essex   Mercia

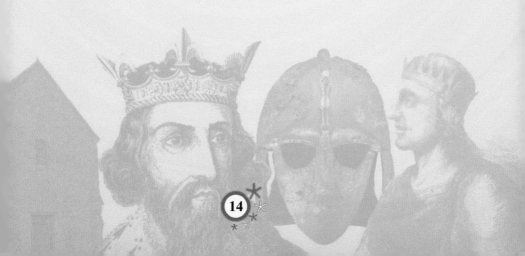

14

Chapter 3: Life in Anglo-Saxon Britain

Life in Anglo-Saxon Britain was very different than life today. The Anglo-Saxons lived in a time without modern technology. They didn't have cars or computers or even a lot of books! They didn't have groceries stores or refrigerators. Can you imagine living in a world without all of these things? Even without the machines and science we have today, the Anglo-Saxons built an impressive culture that still influences our lives.

The Anglo-Saxons did not live in big cities like many of us do in modern times. Instead, most of them were **farmers**. They lived in small **villages** and farmed the land around them. Many villages had less than 100 people in them! Over time, some of the Anglo-Saxons did move into towns, but even their big cities were tiny compared to our cities today. Because the villages were so small and far apart traveling was difficult. Some people traveled, but they had to use bad roads through the forest. Britain used to have abundant forests, but many trees have since been cut down. While traveling the people had to always be careful of wild animals or bandits. Can you imagine traveling everywhere on foot or horseback through the forest? Many people didn't travel far from their village because of how hard traveling was.

The Anglo-Saxons invaded Britain after the Romans left, and the Romans left behind many of their stone cities and roads. It might make sense for the Anglo-Saxons to use those buildings, but they didn't trust the Romans. They decided not to use the Roman buildings and roads—and even destroyed some of them. Instead, the Anglo

Saxons built homes and villages of their own. The Anglo-Saxons built their houses out of wood, and they made **thatched roofs** made from straw or reeds. These houses usually only had one room, and the whole family lived together. Poor families even lived with their animals, but they were usually separated by a screen.

An example of an Anglo-Saxon house.
dun_deagh, CC BY-SA 2.0 <https://creativecommons.org/licenses/by-sa/2.0>, via Wikimedia Commons; https://commons.wikimedia.org/wiki/File:Grubenhaus,_Gearwe,_Bede%27s_World,_Jarrow_(6880268241).jpg

The floors were usually dirt, but wealthy people sometimes had floorboards. Wealthy people also slept on beds, but poor people had to sleep on the dirt floor.

The largest home in the village belonged to the village chief. The chief's house had to be big enough to host all the chief's warriors for big meals. Even though the chief was the wealthiest person in the village, the house was still simple compared to our houses today.

The chief was the most powerful person in the village, but the Anglo-Saxons had a more complicated **social structure**. (A social structure is the way a group of people decides where everyone should be in their group.) The Anglo-Saxons had three main **classes**, or groups of people. The upper class was called the **thanes**. They were rich and spent a lot of time hunting and feasting. The second class was called the **churls**. These were free people, but they didn't have much money. The lowest class was called the **thralls**. These people were slaves, and they lived extremely hard lives. We now know that slavery is wrong, but it was a part of Anglo-Saxon culture.

Most of the Anglo-Saxons took care of themselves by being farmers. They could make tools like plows, and they used animals to help them plow the fields. Farmers grew many different kinds of food. They grew wheat and barley to make bread and porridge and grew vegetables like carrots, parsnips, cabbage, and peas. The Anglo-Saxons also kept herds of animals like sheep, goats, and pigs. In the fall, the Anglo-Saxons would kill some of their animals and preserve the meat by salting it. (Applying salt to meat can keep it from spoiling.) The Anglo-Saxons did this to ensure they had enough food through the winter and to keep their flocks healthy during the cold season.

Not everyone was a farmer. Some people were **craftsmen**. They took jobs as **blacksmiths**, **potters**, and **leather workers**. When working with metal, the Anglo-Saxons made beautiful and detailed jewelry. When working with pottery, the Anglo-Saxons made pots and vessels. At first, they made everything by hand, but in the seventh century, they began using the **pottery wheel**. This might not seem important to us today, but at the time, it completely changed how the Anglo-Saxons made their pottery.

Of course, the Anglo-Saxons focused on many things other than their jobs. They worshipped their own gods at first but eventually converted to Christianity. They built churches near their villages and towns. (We still have some of these buildings today!) The Anglo-Saxons took a long time to completely convert to Christianity, so some of their churches had elements of their old religion inside them too.

St. Peter's Chapel (an Anglo-Saxon church).

The family was also very important to the Anglo-Saxons. Men tended to do the farming or work in craft shops. Women tended to stay home and take care of the house. That included making all the clothes. This may seem limiting to us, but Anglo-Saxon women had their own rights. In their free time, people would hunt, ride horses, and play musical instruments. Their favorite pastime was telling stories or riddles. Many of these stories were passed from person to person and were an important part of their culture. The most famous Anglo-Saxon story is called **Beowulf**. It's a story about a great hero named Beowulf who fights a monster called **Grendel**.

Kids in Anglo-Saxon Britain had to work hard. They didn't have schools like we have today. Can you imagine not having to go to school? They didn't get to play all day, though! The boys learned how to farm or make crafts from their fathers, and the girls learned how to make clothes and take care of the house from their mothers. It was a lot of work, but kids also had free time, just like the adults. The kids had toys like carved horses and board games that they played when they didn't have to work.

The clothes that the Anglo-Saxons wore were different than our clothes. Everything was made from natural fibers like wool. Men wore tunics and a type of trousers called **breeches**. They held their breeches up with a leather belt. When it was cold, the men also wore cloaks. Women wore long linen garments and long tunics over that garment. While both men and women wore clasps and brooches to keep their garments fastened properly, women sometimes wore beaded necklaces, bracelets, and rings.

Life in Anglo-Saxon Britain was different from our lives, but they still worked really hard. Their hard work helped build the country we know, helping us move towards a time when we can travel safely, shop at grocery stores, and attend school. The Anglo-Saxons had complex society, even though we might think they had hard lives when we look back through history.

Chapter 3 Challenge Activity

Villages   Beowulf   clothes

Famers   thatched roofs

The Anglo-Saxons lived very different lives than we do today. They lived in small - _____, and they did not travel a lot. Most of the Anglo-Saxons were _____ and grew their own food, like wheat and carrots. They lived in one-room buildings with _____. The whole family lived together, and everyone worked. Even the kids worked by learning how to farm or make _____, but they still had time to play. The Anglo-Saxons loved telling stories, and one of their most famous stories is _____ .

Chapter 4: Religion and Customs

The religion of Britain changed a lot during the time of the Anglo-Saxons. The main religion changed from pagan to Christianity, but the change wasn't smooth or instant. Even though missionaries began arriving in 597 CE, converting all of the Anglo-Saxons would take many years.

Did you know that there were Christians in Britain before the Anglo-Saxons came? Britain had been ruled by Rome before, and some Romans were Christians. So, some of the Britons converted to Christianity then. When the Anglo-Saxons came to Britain, they brought their **pagan** religion with them. It became the main religion of the land, but we don't know much about it. The Anglo-Saxons did not write down their religious beliefs or customs. They only left some buildings and names, so historians are still trying to figure it out. We do know that there were temples, and some of the temple names are related to names in **Norse mythology**. Norse mythology comes from Northern Germany and Scandinavian areas. They had many different gods. The Anglo-Saxons appear to have worshipped at least some of them.

The Anglo-Saxon pagan religion was the main religion in Britain for a while. Finally, the Christian Church decided to send **missionaries**. (A missionary is someone who goes to a new place and teaches people about their religion. Missionaries want to convince other people to join their religion.) The Christian Church decided to send a monk named **Saint Augustine**.

You may have heard of a different Christian thinker named **Augustine of Hippo**. He lived from 354 to 430 CE and wrote important books about **theology**. (Theology is the study of God.) Some of his books were *Confessions* and *City of God*.

The Augustine who went to Britain was a different man. He eventually became known as Augustine of Canterbury. We don't know much about St. Augustine, but we do know that he lived in the sixth and seventh centuries. He was a monk at St. Andrew's Abbey in Rome.

It wasn't Saint Augustine's idea to go to Britain. **Pope Gregory I** wanted to convert the Anglo-Saxons in Britain to Christianity. Some stories say Pope Gregory saw a couple of light-haired slaves for sale in Rome. When he asked who they were, he was told they were Angles. Pope Gregory said that they were angels, not angles. He decided that the Anglo-Saxons needed to have Christianity.

Pope Gregory chose Kent as the first place Augustine would spread Christianity. One reason he chose Kent was that it was a powerful kingdom in the late sixth century. Pope Gregory I knew that Kent could convince other kingdoms to convert to Christianity. Another reason is that **King Æthelberht** (Ethel-bert) had married a princess named **Bertha**. Bertha was already a Christian, and King Ethelberht allowed her to continue practicing her religion.

Augustine arrived in Kent in 597 CE with about 40 people. King Ethelberht listened to what they had to say and allowed them to settle near **Canterbury**, the capital of Kent. They preached in the city and began to convert many people. The king even converted, although historians are not sure when. Augustine eventually became the first **Archbishop of Canterbury**, which is still a powerful position in the Catholic Church today.

Augustine also started a monastery. He intended it to be dedicated to St. Peter and St. Paul, but he died on May 26, 604 CE, before the monastery was finished. Today, it is known as **St. Augustine's Abbey**, and it is where he is buried. When he died, the Christian mission was still in Kent, but his example soon helped other missionaries convert other parts of Anglo-Saxon Britain.

Augustine of Canterbury's burial site.
https://commons.wikimedia.org/wiki/File:AgCant-tomb.jpg

Of course, St. Augustine was not the only Christian missionary to come to the British Isles. Before St. Augustine went to Britain, missionaries had already begun visiting **Ireland**. One of the most famous missionaries to Ireland was **St. Patrick**. He was born in Britain but was captured by the Irish. He had to work as a herdsman for six years. After escaping, St. Patrick had a dream that told him to return to Ireland and convert people to Christianity.

Historians don't know the exact dates that St. Patrick worked in Ireland, but they believe he was there during the fifth century CE. Later, other missionaries came to Britain from Ireland and helped convert the people there as well.

Other missionaries came to Britain and slowly moved through the Anglo-Saxon kingdoms. There were setbacks as different kings came to power, but Christianity soon spread to Northumbria, Mercia, Wessex, and Sussex. Paganism continued to be a prominent part of Anglo-Saxon life for years, so there was a time when Christianity and Anglo-Saxon pagan practices coexisted. The Venerable Bede even talks about one temple that had both a pagan idol and a Christian church! It belonged to King Rædwald (Reed-wald) of East Anglia in the seventh century.

Æthelstan presenting a Bible to Cuthbert.
https://commons.wikimedia.org/wiki/File:Athelstan.jpg

Christianity had a big impact on the Anglo-Saxons. It changed not only their religious practices but also their **politics** and **culture**. One of the biggest changes was bringing a **system of writing**. (A system of writing is a uniform way that people can write things down.)

You might not think about it much, but someone had to invent the alphabet so we could create words out of the letters. Once we write things down, other people can read the information later. Can you imagine living in a society that couldn't write things down? Communicating would be harder, especially with people far away!

The Anglo-Saxons did not have a system of writing. When the Christian missionaries came, they brought the **Latin** language and the Latin alphabet with them. Kings used the new writing system to write law codes and property charters. It helped to stabilize the Anglo-Saxon kingdoms.

The Christian missionaries also built monasteries in Britain. A **monastery** is a place where monks or nuns live, but back in Anglo-Saxon Britain, monasteries were more than that. They were also important **centers of learning**. They had big libraries because the monks had time to copy books. Back then, books were very expensive because they had to be copied by hand. (The printing press hadn't been invented yet.) The monks took the time to copy many books and were famous for creating beautiful art in the margins of their copies. Because they had so many books, monasteries were also **schools** and **economic centers**. Monasteries were an important part of the Anglo-Saxon church, but experienced some reforms. The most famous reform focused on the **Rule of St. Benedict**. These rules tried to make British monasteries more like ones in Europe, but not all the smaller monasteries followed them.

An 8th-century copy of the rule of St. Benedict.

Christianity had a big impact on the Anglo-Saxons. It gave them a system of writing, a new culture, and a new structure in their society. (The Church had a **hierarchy**, which is a way of ranking people to do certain jobs. The modern Catholic Church has a hierarchy similar to the one the Anglo-Saxons used in their churches.) By converting to Christianity, the Anglo-Saxons had more ties to the rest of Europe. It changed the way the Anglo-Saxons thought about the world around them forever.

Can you answer these questions in complete sentences?

1. In what year did St. Augustine come to Britain?

2. What was the main religion in Britain before the arrival of St. Augustine?

3. Which saint went to Ireland?

4. Why were monasteries important in Anglo-Saxon Britain?

5. What writing system did the missionaries bring with them?

Chapter 5: Alfred the Great

The Anglo-Saxons had many kings during their time in Britain, but the most famous Anglo-Saxon king was **King Alfred the Great**, the king of Wessex from 871 to 899 CE. He stopped the Viking invasion and started bringing all the Anglo-Saxon kingdoms together.

AELFREDUS
MAGNUS

Alfred the Great.
https://commons.wikimedia.org/wiki/File:Alfred_the_Great.jpg

Alfred was born in 849 CE in a town called **Wantage** in Wessex. He was the son of **King Æthelwulf** (Ethel-wolf), but no one expected Alfred to ever be king. They all thought his brothers would rule instead. Alfred had four older brothers!

Historians don't have much information about Alfred's childhood. They know that he visited the pope with his father. They also know that Alfred was sickly. He had health problems his entire life. We don't know what Alfred suffered from, but some historians think it was Crohn's disease. Even though he was probably not physically strong, he was very smart and was good at leading his people.

While Alfred's father and brothers were ruling Wessex, Britain was suffering from Viking attacks. The **Vikings** were people from northern Europe, including modern-day Scandinavia. They were not a united country. Instead, they were a bunch of tribes who shared a similar culture. Some Vikings were farmers, but it was so cold in Scandinavia that they couldn't grow all the food they needed. So, some Vikings were also **raiders**. They attacked towns near coastlines or rivers. The Vikings had shallow boats that allowed them to sail up rivers, and their attacks were so fast that people didn't have time to defend themselves.

The Vikings had been attacking Britain since the 790s. Soon, they didn't just want to raid the cities. They wanted to take Britain for themselves. The Anglo-Saxons didn't want the Vikings to take their land, but the Vikings were so strong that the Anglo-Saxon kingdoms fell one by one. Several of Alfred's brothers died in the battles with the Vikings. By 870 CE, Wessex was the only Anglo-Saxon kingdom left.

Alfred led the Wessex army against the Vikings and became king in 871. He fought against the Vikings and stopped them from taking Wessex. He thought that he had finally achieved peace.

Suddenly, in 878 CE, the Danish **King Guthrum** attacked King Alfred. The attack was so fast that Alfred didn't have time t defend himself or his people. He barely escaped with his life! Can you imagine how scary that must have been for King Alfred? He was scared, but he was also angry. He didn't want the Vikings to take his kingdom away from him.

There's a legend that comes from King Alfred's escape. The legend says that while he was escaping, he stayed at a poor woman's cottage one night. She didn't know he was the king. She was busy working and asked Alfred to watch the cakes she was baking. The king was so busy worrying about his kingdom that he forgot to watch the cakes, and they burned! The poor woman was upset that he let the cakes burn, and she scolded him for it.

King Alfred hid in the Somerset tidal marshes for several months. He gathered a whole army around him, filled with other Anglo-Saxons who wanted to fight back against the Vikings. Many of the people who helped him were local noblemen, like thegns and ealdormen. These people also controlled small groups in the army, so they were still loyal to King Alfred. Finally, in May, King Alfred attacked the Vikings in the **Battle of Edington**. He surprised them using Viking fighting tactics and won! After winning the battle, he followed them to **Chippenham**, which the Vikings were using as a fortress. He laid **siege** to the fortress and forced the Vikings to surrender. The big Viking attack against Wessex was finally over.

King Alfred knew the Vikings were too strong to drive out of Britain completely, so he made an official peace treaty with them. It was called the **Treaty of Wedmore**. The Vikings had to convert to Christianity as part of the treaty, but the most important part of the treaty was that it divided up Britain. The Vikings were given the northern and eastern parts of Britain, and their land was called **Danelaw**. King Alfred kept Wessex and also took over west Mercia and Kent. Dividing up the land meant that everything not under Viking control was under King Alfred's rule. This is how King Alfred became known as the **King of the English**. The Vikings and King Alfred did not always get along after this treaty, but there was a time of relative peace in Britain. King Alfred helped keep the peace by having soldiers guard the border between Danelaw and the Anglo-Saxon lands.

Alfred the Great silver coin. The fact that he is on coinage highlights his importance

King Alfred was a good king during war, but he was an even better king during peaceful times. Because the Vikings weren't gone, one of the first things King Alfred did was reorganize his army and creat strong settlements. These strong settlements were designed t protect people from Viking attacks, and they were built all ove southern Britain. There was even one built in London! The army wa restructured to allow some soldiers to guard the borders whil others cared for their farms.

He also built a navy for Wessex. This was not the first navy in Britain, but it was very important for defending Alfred's land from Viking attacks. He wanted to have power at sea so that he could stop the Vikings before they even arrived.

In addition to working hard to defend his people from the Vikings, King Alfred also created new laws and focused on restarting education. While the Vikings were attacking, many people stopped visiting teachers or learning how to read. You might think that not having class would be fun, but King Alfred knew that not learning at all would be hard. School is where you learn how to think, read, write, and look carefully at the world around you. These are important skills for any person to have, and King Alfred knew his people needed them to survive future Viking attacks and build a strong kingdom.

King Alfred started schools and helped rebuild monasteries. To help resupply all the books the Vikings had destroyed, Alfred even helped translate the books he thought were most important from Latin to Anglo-Saxon.

King Alfred died in 899 CE. He was only 50 years old! King Alfred the Great is most famous for stopping the Vikings and uniting the remaining Anglo-Saxon kingdoms. He helped pave the way for Britain's unification under one king. Because of his hard work and dedication to his kingdom, King Alfred is the only British king called the Great." It helps us remember that King Alfred the Great moved Britain towards the country it is today.

Can you put these events in the correct order?

- ➤ The Vikings first invade Britain.

- ➤ Alfred restarts schools in Wessex.

- ➤ The Treaty of Wedmore is signed.

- ➤ Alfred is born in Wantage.

- ➤ Alfred becomes king.

- ➤ Alfred burns a poor woman's cakes, according to legend.

Chapter 6: King Offa and Egbert

Both King Offa and King Egbert are famous Anglo-Saxon kings, even though they come from different kingdoms. Let's look at what made each king important and how they shaped the Anglo-Saxons in Britain.

King Offa

King Offa was the king of **Mercia** from 757 to 796 CE. He was one of the most powerful Anglo-Saxon kings, and he ruled Mercia while it was the strongest kingdom in Britain. King Offa was so powerful that he had even worked with European rulers like **Charlemagne**! Charlemagne was an important ruler in France during this time, so it was a big deal that he traded with King Offa.

Historians don't know much about Offa before he became king. His father was **Thingfrith** (thing-frith), but he wasn't the king. The king of Mercia was **King Æthelbald** (ethel-bald), but he was murdered in 757 CE. Several people wanted the throne, and they all fought each other in a brief civil war. Finally, Offa won and became king in 757 CE.

King Offa expanded his power by taking over other Anglo-Saxon kingdoms nearby. He soon had Kent, Essex, and Sussex under his power. King Offa even had influence in other kingdoms like Wessex and East Anglia! This influence meant he could put anyone he wanted on their thrones. (Can you imagine having so much power that you could tell other countries who their rulers would be?) King Offa didn't ever unite all of the Anglo-Saxons, but he did start calling himself the **Bretwalda of England**. Bretwalda (bret-wall-da) means overlord. While he was king of Mercia, King Offa controlled much of England. He was known for being ruthless, creative, and determined.

During this time in history, being a powerful king wasn't just about having a strong army. You also had to have good marriages. It might seem strange to us, but many royal people did not marry for love. They married for political power. King Offa did the same thing. He arranged marriages for his daughters with kings in Northumbria and Wessex. He even offered to arrange a marriage between his children and Charlemagne's children, but Charlemagne didn't agree to it.

King Offa is most famous for constructing **Offa's Dyke**. A dyke is a defense system made of dirt, a manmade hill with a ditch on one side. The ditch would be dug on the side away from your kingdom. Dykes made it harder for people who wanted to invade your kingdom to climb over the hill, and it gave you a good place to defend your borders. Offa's Dyke was built between Mercia and **Wales** to keep the Welsh out. The dyke was 140 miles long, and you can still see parts of it today! It runs along the border between England and Wales.

An image of a coin with Offa, king of Mercia 757-796.
https://commons.wikimedia.org/wiki/File:Offa_king_of_Mercia_757_796.jpg

King Offa was a powerful king who led Mercia through its most powerful time. However, his work didn't last long after he died in 796. He wanted his son **Ecgfrith** (ec-frith) to take over, but Ecgfrith was killed before he had ruled for a year. A lot of Offa's work unraveled, and Mercia fell from power, never again to rule Britain as it had with Offa.

King Offa is remembered for his defensive dyke, his energy, and his ability to bring many of the other Anglo-Saxon kingdoms under his power.

King Egbert

King Egbert is the second most famous king from Wessex. He is famous for bringing together Wessex's power and overthrowing Mercia's power. Some historians believe that Egbert's work helped Wessex successfully fight against the Vikings.

Egbert was born around 770 CE, but historians don't know much about his childhood. They don't even know if he was born in Kent or Wessex! When King Cynewulf (kin-e-wolf) of Wessex died in 786 CE, Egbert wanted the throne. The problem was that he wasn't the only one. **Beorhtric** (be-or-dric) also had a claim to the throne, and he asked King Offa to support him. At the time, King Offa was the most powerful king in all of Britain, and he made sure that Beorhtric became the next king of Wessex. Egbert was banished from Britain, so he went to France to live with **Emperor Charlemagne** for a few years. Egbert married a noblewoman named **Redburga**, and he stayed in France until 802 CE. Beorhtric died in 802, so Egbert returned to Wessex and became the next king. He probably had Charlemagne's help, but the people of Wessex seem to have accepted him.

Portrait of Egbert.
https://commons.wikimedia.org/wiki/File:Portrait_of_Egbert_(4673108).jpg

Historians don't have much information about the first few years o
King Egbert's reign. They think he spent time building up an army an
restructuring the government. Around 815 CE, Egbert took ove
Cornwall, a region next to Wessex. He probably started wit
Cornwall because it had good metalworking and a strong trad
system. These are important things to have if you are trying to buil
an army.

In 825, Mercia decided to bring Wessex back under its control, so **King Beornwulf** (be-orn-wolf) attacked. This led to the **Battle of Ellandun** (el-ad-dun), one of the most decisive battles in Anglo-Saxon history. King Egbert defeated King Beornwulf! Wessex had finally defeated Mercia. Then, King Egbert marched into Kent and began taking over the kingdoms that Mercia used to rule. Egbert soon had control over Kent, Sussex, Surrey, and East Anglia. In 829, he defeated Mercia itself. The only kingdom left was Northumbria, and it quickly accepted King Egbert as its overlord. In just four years, King Egbert became the **Bretwalda** of Britain.

King Egbert didn't have the resources to control all of Britain for long. By 831, Mercia had broken free of his control once again and was ruling itself independently. Also, the Vikings began to threaten the British coasts. Egbert spent the rest of his reign battling against the Vikings, and he died in 839 CE.

King Egbert was the most powerful king during his time. He oversaw the power shift from Mercia to Wessex, and his work helped prepare Wessex to survive the coming Viking attacks. Although Egbert could not bring all of England together as one kingdom, his power helped stabilize Wessex, creating the foundation that kings like King Alfred the Great would use to unite the Anglo-Saxons into one kingdom.

Can you match the following facts to the correct king?

King Offa	King Egbert

King of Mercia

Constructed a dyke between England and Wales

Lived in Charlemagne's court for a few years

Won the Battle of Ellandun

Became king after King Æthelbald

Became overlord of Northumbria

King of Wessex

Arranged marriages to get better political power

Chapter 7: Who Were the Normans?

The Normans were the last people to successfully invade Britain. They officially conquered the Anglo-Saxons in 1066, and their invasion would once again change the course of British history. The Anglo-Saxons were still part of British life. By combining the Norman and Anglo-Saxon cultures, the people created a new culture that would eventually result in modern English culture. Part of that new culture was a new language we now call **Old English**. We have a lot of modern things that came from the Norman invasion of Britain!

It's important to note that the Normans were not the same people as the Vikings. The Vikings had been attacking England for several hundred years and had even taken over part of it. The Normans came from an area of France called **Normandy**. They were related to the Vikings, though.

The Vikings had been raiding Europe for a few hundred years, and that included France. The attacks on France were fierce because France had lots of resources. They soon took some land of their own near the end of the **Seine River** (sane). In 911, King Charles III made a treaty with a Viking ruler named **Rollo**. Rollo was already famous for his invasions of Ireland and Scotland, and some stories say he was so large that a horse couldn't carry him. He might have been big, but many other rulers were definitely afraid of him!

King Charles III gave Rollo some land in northern France around the mouth of the Seine River. This area was Normandy. Rollo became the first **Duke of Normandy**, and the Vikings there quickly began adapting to the French language and customs. Within 100 years, the Normans were a separate group from the Vikings. That's a really short amount of time, especially in history!

Can you imagine changing your entire language and culture in just a few years?

The Normans spoke ancient French and converted to Christianity. They became well-known for being adaptive. Just like the Vikings, they could travel across land or sea quickly. But unlike the Vikings, the Normans also learned how to fight on horseback, and they spread **feudalism** to every place they conquered.

Feudalism was a social structure that provided a lot of structure to medieval society. At the top was the king. The king owned all the land, but he gave land to the nobility. The nobility agreed to give the king military support during wars in exchange for land. The nobility then passed out parts of the land to **vassals**. Vassals were people who agreed to serve the nobility in exchange for land and protection. This kind of structure went all the way down to the peasants. Peasants lived on a noble's land and either helped work it or gave the nobility some of the harvest. In exchange for all this work, the nobility protected the peasants from enemy armies.

The Normans also adopted a lot of other things from the French. They learned how to fight on horses and soon became experts at it just like many other kingdoms in Europe. They used the same type of horse as the French. They even wore armor similar to that of other soldiers in northwestern Europe! They wore a shirt called a **hauberk** (how-berk) made out of chain mail (a type of armor made out of small metal rings). This made it flexible enough to fight in but also helped protect the soldier from arrows and swords. It usually reached from the neck down to mid-thigh, but there were some differences from person to person.

The Normans also wore a helmet shaped like a cone and carried a shield shaped like a diamond. They had both a long sword and lance to fight with. Both weapons were good to use on horseback, and the Normans became famous for being the most powerful on the battlefield. They were strong and ruthless and quickly adapted to the environment and culture around them. They even traveled as far away as **Italy** and **Sicily**, where they started their conquest by hiring themselves out as mercenaries. (A **mercenary** is a soldier for hire. Mercenaries will fight for whoever will pay them the most money.) There were eventually so many Normans in Italy and Sicily that they took some land for themselves.

Bayeux Tapestry depicts a Norman siege on an Anglo-Saxon.
https://commons.wikimedia.org/wiki/File:Bayeux_Tapestry_scene19_detail_Castle_Dinan.jpg

Of course, the Normans also wanted to conquer Britain. Normandy was a wealthy kingdom already. It had a lot of textile work. **Textiles** another word for fabric, and during this time in history, people had to make fabric so that they could make clothes. The people in Normandy were very good at making fabric, so they sold it and made money that way. However, like many other kingdoms, the Normans wanted to conquer other lands to gain more power and resources.

In 1066, **William the Conqueror** was the Duke of Normandy, and he believed he had a right to the English throne. When **King Edward the Confessor** died, William wanted to be crowned king. The Anglo-Saxons didn't agree with him. They crowned **Harold Godwin** as the next king. William decided to invade and take the throne by force. This started the **Norman Conquest**, and it was the last time England has ever successfully been invaded. The Normans eventually defeated the Anglo-Saxons at the **Battle of Hastings**.

The Anglo-Saxons and the Normans were very different. The Normans brought feudalism with them, but the Anglo-Saxons structured their government using a **shire system** that divided the land into sections. People were appointed to keep order in their shire, but feudalism was more structured than the shire system.

The Normans made the Anglo-Saxon government more efficient and ensured that England was safe from foreign invasions. This helped them unify the country more securely than the Anglo-Saxons had been able to.

The Normans also brought their **architecture** with them. The Anglo-Saxons usually built wooden structures, but the Normans built stone buildings. They liked to build castles on top of hills because those were easier to defend, but they also built stone churches and monasteries. These buildings were more permanent than the Anglo Saxon buildings. They were impressive and had to be noticed, just like the Norman people.

The Normans needed only 100 years to build a unique culture that allowed them to conquer places all over Europe, but their most famous conquest was in Britain. They defeated the Anglo-Saxon people and moved Britain into the next phase of its history. We continue to be influenced today by the results of Norman spirit and determination that took root in Anglo-Saxon Britain.

Chapter 7 Challenge Activity

Can you answer the following questions in complete sentences?

1. Who was the first Duke of Normandy?

   _____

   _____

2. What is feudalism?

   _____

   _____

3. What kind of armor did the Normans wear?

   _____

   _____

4. How was Old English invented?

   _____

   _____

5. How did the Anglo-Saxons structure their society? Was it different tha
   feudalism?

   _____

   _____

6. When did William the Conqueror invade England?

   _____

   _____

Chapter 8: The Battle of Hastings

The **Battle of Hastings** is one of the most important battles in British history. It was the decisive battle in the **Norman Conquest**, and the Norman victory marked the end of Anglo-Saxon rule in Britain.

But how did this battle even begin?

The Norman Conquest began when **King Edward the Confessor** died in 1066. He didn't have any children, so everyone was uncertain about who the next king should be. There were three men who thought they had the best claim to the throne of England.

The first man was **King Harald Hardrada** (harold hard-ra-da) of Norway. He thought that the Vikings should have the throne. They had held the throne earlier but had lost it to the Anglo-Saxons before King Edward. When King Edward died without children, King Harald Hardrada thought it was time for the Vikings to take the throne again.

The second man was **Harold Godwinson**. He was the Earl of Wessex and King Edward's brother-in-law. Harold was a powerful man, and he was accepted by the Anglo-Saxons as the next king.

The third man was **William of Normandy**. He is more famously known as William the Conqueror. William was King Edward's cousin, and he claimed that Edward had made him the heir. (This means Edward had promised the English throne would go to William after his death.) He also said that Harold Godwinson had promised to support William's claim to the throne in 1065. Historians are not sure if this is true, but if Harold did offer to support William's claim, he went back on his word in 1066. This made William very angry, so he decided to invade Britain.

While William was preparing to invade Britain, King Harald Hardrada was also planning to invade. Hardrada arrived first, and King Harold of England met him at **Stamford Bridge** in north England. This battle was fierce and deadly. King Harold Godwinson's own brother even supported the Norwegian king instead of him! His brother's name was **Tostig** (tos-tig). Can you imagine fighting a big battle against your own sibling? By the end of the battle, over 5,000 people had died, including King Harald Hardrada and Tostig. The threat of the Norwegian king taking the English throne was over.

Sample of Anglo-Saxon gear for battle.
https://creativecommons.org/publicdomain/zero/1.0/ , https://pxhere.com/en/photo/615382

However, the threat of Normandy taking the throne was still very real. William of Normandy arrived in southern England with his army and King Harold of England had to march down to meet him. The met at Hastings to battle over who should have the English throne.

The battle only lasted one day. It took place on October 14, 1066. King Harold had more soldiers, but William's soldiers had more energy. The English soldiers quickly got into formation behind a shield wall on a hill. This shield wall kept the Normans back for a while. William's **cavalry** couldn't break through the shield wall because they were fighting uphill. (A cavalry is a group of soldiers who fight on horses.) Can you imagine how hard it would be to run uphill with all of that armor on? It's no wonder the horses couldn't move fast enough to break through a shield wall!

The Anglo-Saxons also had two-handed **battleaxes**. These weapons were designed to cut through armor like chainmail, so the Normans had some problems at the beginning of the battle. William knew that if he wanted to win, he needed to rethink his strategy.

Battlefield of the Battle of Hastings.

William knew he needed to break through the Anglo-Saxon shield wall, so he did two things. First, he told his archers to stop shooting arrows at the shield. Instead, he told them to shoot their arrows high above the shields. This made the arrows come down onto the Anglo-Saxons. One of these arrows actually killed King Harold! It struck him through his eye, and he died. The Anglo-Saxons didn't stop fighting, though. They wanted to defend their fallen king and get rid of the invaders.

The second thing William did was to tell his soldiers to pretend to retreat. This is an old battle strategy called **feigned flight** that many leaders have used. The winning side will usually chase the people who are retreating, which means they will break their formation. If you really are winning, it's not a problem. If it's a trick, it leaves you vulnerable to attacks. William of Normandy tricked the Anglo-Saxons into taking down their shield wall by pretending to retreat.

Once the shield wall was broken, the Normans turned back and fought the Anglo-Saxons fiercely. By the end of the day, the battle was over. The Anglo-Saxon soldiers were either dead or running for their lives. William of Normandy had won the Battle of Hastings.

This wasn't the last battle in the Norman Conquest, but it was the most important. William still had to fight his way to London. Not all of the Anglo-Saxon soldiers had come to the Battle of Hastings, so there were little armies all along the way. The Anglo-Saxons did not want to accept William as their new king, but he overpowered all resistance. William was crowned King of England on Christmas Day in 1066.

Tomb of Duke of Normandy.
Poliphilo, CC0, via Wikimedia Commons;
https://commons.wikimedia.org/wiki/File:Tomb_of_Robert,_Duke_of_Normandy,_Gloucester_Cathedral_02.jpg

The Battle of Hastings was an important turning point in English history. Norman rule changed everything from politics to religion to language. The changes that the Normans made to the religious structures in England would later impact all Christian churches around the world.

After becoming king, William the Conqueror built an abbey next to the battle site. It was called **Battle Abbey**. Some historians think Pope Alexander II ordered him to build the abbey as penance (a punishment) for invading, but others think William had already promised to build an abbey if he won the battle. Either way, you can still visit Battle Abbey today in England.

William also made a lot of new laws and wrote a document called the **Doomsday Book**. It's a document that details the landowners in England and what they owned. Many Anglo-Saxon nobles had fled the country, so he needed a way to keep track of who owned the land. This was a big deal at the time, and it helped William set up a better tax system. William also changed the official language of the court to **French**. It was the only language he spoke, and it added hundreds of French words to the Anglo-Saxon language. This eventually created Old English.

The Norman Conquest changed a lot in England, and the Norman influence in England continues to impact the world. The Normans added structure to the kingdom and used force whenever a group of Anglo-Saxons rebelled. England would never be the same, and it all changed in one day at the Battle of Hastings.

Chapter 8 Challenge Activity

Can you solve the crossword puzzle below?

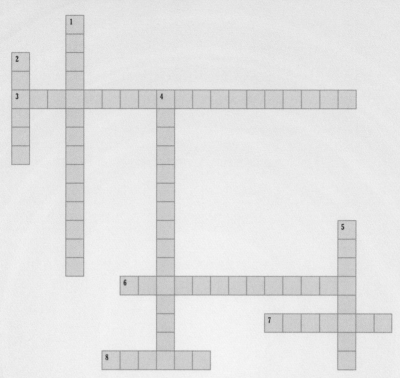

DOWN

1. King _____ was the Norwegian king who also wanted the English throne.

2. Which king was known as the Confessor?

4. Who was crowned king after King Edward died?

5. The Battle of _____ was fought on October 14, 1066.

ACROSS

3. Who was the victor of the Battle of Hastings?

6. The battle tactic called _____ helped the Normans break through the Anglo-Saxon shield wall.

7. The Normans were related to which European group?

8. What was the official language of William's court?

Chapter 9: Art, Literature, and Artifacts

The Anglo-Saxons had a lot going on during their time in Britain. They found new land, created new kingdoms, converted to a new religion, and fought against the Vikings. But even though they were busy, the Anglo-Saxons also made time to create beautiful art. They worked in many different areas of art, and some of these pieces are in museums for you to see today!

One area of art the Anglo-Saxons focused on was metalworking. Did you know there is more to metalworking than just making swords or horseshoes? The Anglo-Saxons made beautiful and delicate things out of metal.

Anglo-Saxon metalwork.

The Anglo-Saxons are famous for their work on **jewelry** and **brooches.** The pieces are very detailed. Some pieces are so intricate that experts are still trying to figure out how the Anglo Saxons made them without a magnifying glass! We have a lot o different pieces of Anglo-Saxon metalwork because they tended to place it on burial sites. They believed it was important to bury the dead with everything they might need, including jewelry. Burying people with jewelry was more common before the Anglo-Saxons converted to Christianity, but even afterward, they still made beautiful art out of metal.

The Anglo-Saxons worked in a lot of different **mediums**. A medium in art is the material used or the way that you create the art. Metalwork is one medium, and **textiles** are another. Fabric and weaving were an art form and a way to tell stories. Art historians usually say that the **Bayeux Tapestry** (bai-oo) is one of the best pieces of Anglo-Saxon art. It's technically embroidered, not woven. Tapestries have the pattern woven into the fabric itself. Embroidery is when someone sews the pattern on top of the fabric after the fabric is woven together. However, it is still called a tapestry. Many other embroidered pieces from the early medieval ages are also conventionally called tapestries.

Even though the Bayeux Tapestry is not woven, it is still impressive. It's 224.3 feet long! Can you imagine creating something over 200 feet long by hand? It's only 1.6 feet wide, but it's still almost three-fourths of a football field. The Bayeux Tapestry tells the story of the Norman Conquest, and it has notes in Latin to explain the pictures. The yarns used were colors like dull red, olive green, blue, and dull gold. Although it was ordered by the Normans, it was still made by Anglo-Saxon artists. That's why the Bayeux Tapestry is still considered Anglo-Saxon art, and it is one of the best pieces they made.

Bayeux Tapestry.
https://commons.wikimedia.org/wiki/File:Odo_bayeux_tapestry.png

Another form of art in Anglo-Saxon culture was literature. The Anglo-Saxons wrote many stories, and they loved to tell stories. As you may remember from Chapter 3, one of the most famous Anglo-Saxon stories is called *Beowulf* (Bay-o-wolf). It is written as an **epic**. (An epic is a long poem about big adventures.) This story is about a warrior named Beowulf who visits a king named Hrothgar (her-oath-gar) at his big mead hall. This was an important place for warriors to gather. There, Hrothgar tells Beowulf about a monster named **Grendel**, who attacks Hrothgar and his men every night. Beowulf fights Grendel and defeats him.

Historians don't know who first wrote *Beowulf*. They also don't know when it was written, but most believe it was between 608 CE and 1000 CE. The version we have now was written in **Old English**, which is not like our English today. It's much closer to what the

Anglo-Saxons spoke, a language closer to German. When the Anglo-Saxon language mixed with French during the Norman Conquest, people made a new one that combined the two. We call that Old English. If you heard Old English today, you might not be able to understand it.

However, English continued to change. There's another important English work called **The Canterbury Tales**. It was written by **Geoffrey Chaucer** in the 1300s. *The Canterbury Tales* tells about a group of travelers going from London to Canterbury. They were **pilgrims** going on a religious trip. To pass the time as they traveled, they all told stories to each other. Some of the stories are funny, but some are serious. Chaucer planned to have 120 stories, but he only finished twenty-three-and-a-half stories.

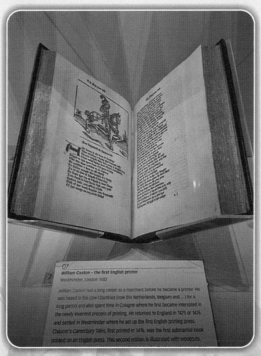

The Canterbury Tales.

Interestingly, *The Canterbury Tales* is not written in Old English. The language had changed so much that historians call this **Middle English**. It's the mid-point between Old English and modern English. You might not be able to read Middle English without help, but you might understand it if it was read to you. Some words would sound strange, but you might also be surprised how much you can learn by studying how the English language has changed over time.

The Anglo-Saxons also copied books, but they didn't just copy the words. They also illustrated the books as they copied them to create **illuminated manuscripts**. This is probably the most famous type of Anglo-Saxon art. Illustrated books today usually have pictures that accompany the story. These picture books can be very pretty, but Anglo-Saxon illuminated manuscripts were much more than just picture books.

The Anglo-Saxons drew in the margins and also decorated the margins and even some of the letters with patterns, bright colors, and gold. Some of the patterns that the Anglo-Saxons used to decorate their manuscripts were already used in their metalwork. Illuminated manuscripts were usually copies of the books in the Bible. Popular books were the **Gospels** and **Psalms**. Many artists who created the illuminated manuscripts were monks living in monasteries.

Did you know that there were different types of illuminated manuscripts? These ways of creating this art form are called **schools**. Before the Norman Conquest, there was a small school in Canterbury and a big one in Northumbria. These illuminated manuscripts had lots of colors and complicated patterns. After the Norman Conquest, the **Winchester school of illumination** became very popular. It was connected to Canterbury and used strong colors and lots of gold. The artists put a lot of time and effort into the illuminated manuscripts, showing how important they thought the books were.

Anglo-Saxon art continues to amaze people today. They put a lot of details into their work, whether metal, fabric, or paint. The Anglo-Saxons were dedicated and sophisticated in their art. Although English art changed after the Norman Conquest, the Anglo-Saxon way of art continues to be part of English culture.

Chapter 9 Challenge Activity

Can you match the art piece to its name?

Illuminated manuscript •   •

Bayeux Tapestry •   •

Canterbury Tales •   •

Alfred Jewel •   •

The Anglo-Saxons made a huge impact on Britain. Throughout this book, we've looked at many parts of Anglo-Saxon life, and they were all important in making Britain the country that it is today. Can you imagine how different life might be today if the Anglo-Saxons had never come to Britain?

One of the Anglo-Saxon legacies was their religion. The Anglo-Saxons arrived as pagans, but by the 500s CE, **Pope Gregory** was determined to spread Christianity to the edge of the known world. Today, we don't think of England being far away from anything, but back then, people didn't know if anything was beyond it. In 597 CE, **Saint Augustine** landed in Kent and started converting the Anglo-Saxons to Christianity.

Æthelberht of Kent sculpture on Canterbury Cathedral.

Once they were converted to Christianity, the Anglo-Saxons were focused on their new religion. They built churches, made art, and argued theology. All of their work changed how other people practiced Christianity throughout Europe.

Anglo-Saxon church at Escomb.

But the Anglo-Saxons did more than just build churches. Did you know that the Anglo-Saxons translated the first English Gospels? Although the church in Rome said that Christian services needed to be spoken in Latin, not everyone understood Latin. The Anglo-Saxons wanted to change that. Some historians believe **King Æthelstan** (Ethel-stan) asked for a translation of the Gospels. He wanted it in the **vernacular** language, which means the language that most people speak every day. For him, that was Anglo-Saxon. Centuries before people were fighting about translating the Bible out of Latin, the Anglo-Saxons had already translated the Gospels. It became an important text for the growing English culture.

The Anglo-Saxons weren't only interested in Christianity. They wanted knowledge and wisdom from anywhere they could get it. They learned grammar, poetry, and theology from **Theodore of Tarsus**, who was from Syria, and **Hadrian**, who was from Libya. The monks wanted to copy as many books as possible, even if the book wasn't religious. The Anglo-Saxons were so focused on learning that some even became international scholars! The most famous one was named **Alcuin** (al-co-in). He worked for Charlemagne in France for some time because Charlemagne was so impressed by his work.

The Anglo-Saxons helped keep books and ideas safe. Some of the books they translated were lost in other libraries, so we wouldn't have them today without the Anglo-Saxons. Even after the Vikings invaded and burned many of the monasteries, the Anglo-Saxons translated the most important books. They were led by King Alfred the Great, who wanted to restore education in England. They worked together to translate books into Anglo-Saxon so that people could continue learning, even if they were living in hard times. The world would be a less knowledgeable place today if the Anglo-Saxons had not wanted to get as much knowledge as they could. Can you imagine what books and ideas we might have lost if the Anglo-Saxons had not worked so hard to save them?

The Anglo-Saxons also created a lot of books. They are most famous for their **poetry** and their **histories**. But Anglo-Saxon poetry isn't like our poetry. They weren't concerned about rhyming, and their poems are more like **epics**. They tell long stories about battles and great heroes. There are several Anglo-Saxon poems we still have today. One of them is called the *Dream of the Rood*, and it is carved into a giant stone cross in Ruthwell! Anglo-Saxon poems like *Beowulf* laid the foundation for many of the stories we have today, such as *Harry Potter*. Can you imagine a world without these heroic stories?

Histories were another important type of book for the Anglo-Saxons. They wrote several different history books, including *The Ecclesiastical History of the English People* and the *Anglo-Saxon Chronicle*. These books gave us a lot of information about the Anglo-Saxons, and they mark the start of English narrative history.

These histories also show us how the Anglo-Saxons started the idea of one English nation. The Anglo-Saxons first created several little kingdoms, but they eventually came up with the idea of one kingdom. They also made the first laws for all of England. Each kingdom had its own laws, but once the Anglo-Saxons united, they needed to create new laws. The new laws were started by King Æthelstan. He had a lot of ambitions, and his hard work helped make the Anglo-Saxon dream of unity a reality. How different would the world be if the Anglo-Saxons hadn't created a unified England?

Sadly, the Anglo-Saxons did not rule Britain forever. In 1066, the Normans overthrew the Anglo-Saxons, and some historians believe England is still recovering from that invasion.

Anglo-Saxon mask.
https://www.flickr.com/photos/101561334@N08/36398395051

Even though **William the Conqueror** changed most of the ruling class, he kept the local governments. He kept the shires and the towns. People found themselves working for new leaders, and there was tension for many years.

How would you feel if your country was suddenly invaded?

The Anglo-Saxons and Normans did eventually find peace. They became one people with one culture, but all of their issues weren't fixed immediately. The Normans also invaded Wales and Scotland, and people today are still arguing about whether or not these two places should be independent from England.

How would the Norman invasion have been different if the Anglo-Saxons had not been in England? There might not have been the Battle of Hastings. The Normans might have needed to unify England. What else do you think might have been different?

The Anglo-Saxons are important in English history. They worked hard, fought bravely, and valued learning. They also gave England the basic political structure it still uses today. The Anglo-Saxons didn't just shape Britain. Because they copied as many books as possible, they saved books for us that would have been lost otherwise. The Norman Conquest changed English history, but our world is better because of the Anglo-Saxons.

How have the Anglo-Saxons influenced your life? If you look closely, you might be surprised at what great things you find.

Can you answer these true or false questions about the whole book correctly?

1. King Alfred the Great was the king of the Vikings.

2. St. Augustine was a Christian missionary who came to Kent in 597 CE.

3. The most famous Anglo-Saxon story is called Beowulf.

4. The Anglo-Saxons spoke English like we do today.

5. William the Conqueror was a Norman leader from Germany.

6. King Offa was the first king of England.

7. Children did not have public schools in Anglo-Saxon England like we do today.

8. Wessex was the last kingdom standing against the Vikings.

9. The Anglo-Saxons were made of three tribes: the Angles, the Saxons, and the Jutes.

10. The Venerable Bede wrote the Anglo-Saxon Chronicle.

11. The Bayeux Tapestry is one of the best pieces of Anglo-Saxon art.

12. King Alfred helped translate books into Anglo-Saxon to help his people learn more.

Answer Key

Chapter 1

B	B	P	S	R	L	V	O	A	E	I	E	A	N
I	G	R	O	N	O	R	T	H	S	E	A	N	N
M	N	G	A	B	O	A	T	S	N	N	I	V	O
O	I	N	A	N	B	E	D	E	A	I	D	G	R
R	M	M	S	M	I	K	A	U	O	T	O	O	M
G	R	S	E	C	N	I	J	U	T	E	S	O	A
N	A	T	L	S	R	F	N	T	B	M	D	N	N
O	F	R	E	S	O	S	M	G	K	M	E	N	N
X	G	E	G	B	M	J	A	M	D	V	R	P	P
A	S	N	N	R	A	N	B	M	T	O	A	R	S
S	L	F	A	I	N	N	N	T	A	G	M	M	M
I	A	N	N	T	B	P	I	C	T	S	R	A	A
I	T	I	A	O	E	T	F	F	N	N	T	A	S
E	M	E	N	N	R	F	I	T	B	N	A	O	B
				C	N								C

Words found: NORTH SEA, BOATS, JUTES, ROMAN, BRITON, VORTIGERN, ANGLES, SAXONS, PICTS, NORMAN, NORMANS, BEDE

Chapter 2

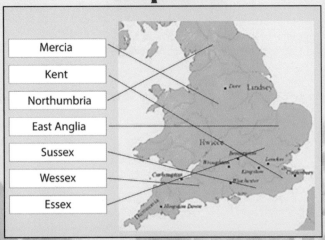

- Mercia
- Kent
- Northumbria
- East Anglia
- Sussex
- Wessex
- Essex

Chapter 3

The Anglo-Saxons lived very different lives than we do today. They lived in small villages, and they did not travel a lot. Most of the Anglo-Saxons were farmers and grew their own food, like wheat and carrots. They lived in one-room buildings with thatched roofs. The whole family lived together, and everyone worked. Even the kids worked by learning how to farm or make clothes, but they still had time to play. The Anglo-Saxons loved telling stories, and one of their most famous stories is Beowulf.

Chapter 4

1. In what year did St. Augustine come to Britian?

   He came to Britain in 597 CE.

2. What was the main religion in Britian before the arrival of St. Augustine?

   The main religion was pagan.

3. Which saint went to Ireland?

   St. Patrick went to Ireland.

4. Why were monasteries important in Anglo-Saxon Britain?

   Monasteries were centers of learning because they had books. They were also economic centers.

5. What writing system did the missionaries bring with them?

   The missionaries brought Latin with them.

Chapter 5

__1_ The Vikings first invade Britain.

__6_ Alfred restarts schools in Wessex.

__5_ The Treaty of Wedmore is signed.

__2_ Alfred is born in Wantage.

___3_ Alfred becomes king.

___4_ Alfred burns a poor woman's cakes, according to legend.

Chapter 6

King Offa	King Egbert
King of Mercia	Lived in Charlemagne's court for a few years
Constructed a dyke between England and Wales	Won the Battle of Ellandun
Became king after King Æthelbald	Became overlord of Northumbria
Arranged marriages to get better political power	King of Wessex

Chapter 7

1. Who was the first Duke of Normany?

   Rollo was the first Duke of Normany.

2. What is feudalism?

   Feudalism is a social structure. The king is at the top and gives land to nobility. The nobility then give land to other people called peasants and promised to protect them from their enemies.

3. What kind of armor did the Normans wear?

   They wore a chain mail shirt called a hauberk. They also wore a helment. They carried a shield, sword, and lance.

4. How was Old English invented?

   Old English was invented when the Normans invaded. Their language mixed with the Anglo-Saxon language to create Old English.

5. How did the Anglo-Saxons structure their society? Was it different than feudalism?

   The Anglo-Saxons used the shire system. Yes, it was different than feudalism because it was less structured.

6. When did William the Conqueror invade England?

   William the Conqueror invaded England in 1066.

Chapter 8

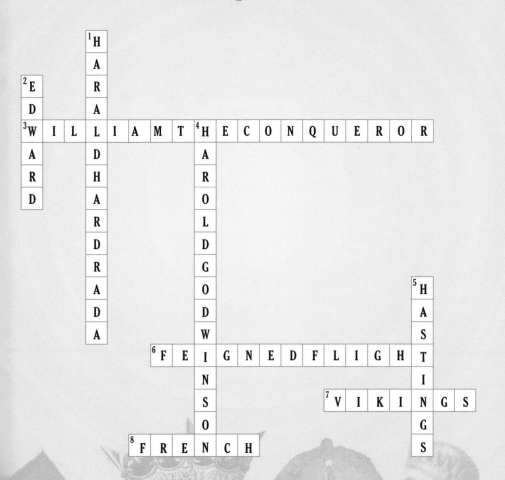

Chapter 9

Illuminated manuscript

https://commons.wikimedia.org/wiki/File:Scorpion_and_snake_
fighting_Anglo-Saxon_c_1050.jpg

Bayeux Tapestry

https://commons.wikimedia.org/wiki/File:Odo_bayeux_tapestry.png

Canterbury Tales

Alfred Jewel

Chapter 10

1. King Alfred the Great was the king of the Vikings. False

2. St. Augustine was a Christian missionary who came to Kent in 597 CE. True

3. The most famous Anglo-Saxon story is called Beowulf. True

4. The Anglo-Saxons spoke English like we do today. False

5. William the Conqueror was a Norman leader from Germany. False

6. King Offa was the first king of England. False

7. Children did not have public schools in Anglo-Saxon England like we do today. True

8. Wessex was the last kingdom standing against the Vikings. True

9. The Anglo-Saxons were made of three tribes: the Angles, the Saxons, and the Jutes. True

10. The Venerable Bede wrote the Anglo-Saxon Chronicle. False

11. The Bayeux Tapestry is one of the best pieces of Anglo-Saxon art. True

12. King Alfred helped translate books into Anglo-Saxon to help his people learn more. True

If you want to learn more about tons of other exciting historical periods, check out our other books!

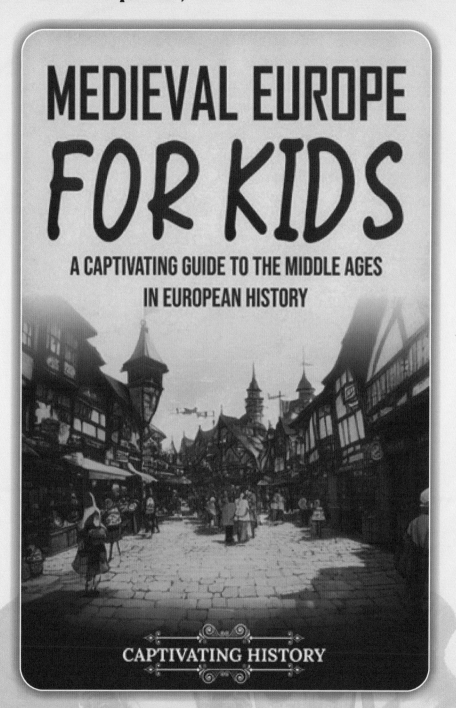

MEDIEVAL EUROPE
FOR KIDS

A CAPTIVATING GUIDE TO THE MIDDLE AGES IN EUROPEAN HISTORY

CAPTIVATING HISTORY

Bibliography

"Alfred the Great (r. 871-899)." *Royal.uk.* Accessed October 2022. https://www.royal.uk/alfred-great-r-871-899.

"Alfred the Great Facts for Kids." *Kiddle Encyclopedia*. July 22, 2022. https://kids.kiddle.co/Alfred_the_Great

"Anglo Saxon Art Facts for Kids." *Elizabethan English Life.com*. Elizabethan Era. Accessed October 2022. https://elizabethanenglandlife.com/anglo-saxons/anglo-saxon-art-facts-for-kids.html

"Augustine of Canterbury." *British Library*. British Library Board. Accessed October 2022. https://www.bl.uk/people/augustine

"Augustine of Canterbury Facts for Kids." *Kiddle Encyclopedia*. August 8, 2022. https://kids.kiddle.co/Augustine_of_Canterbury#:~:text=Augustine%20of%20Canterbury%20(early%206th,founder%20of%20the%20English%20Church

"Awesome Anglo-Saxon Facts!" *National Geographic Kids*. Accessed September 2022. https://www.natgeokids.com/uk/discover/history/general-history/anglo-saxons/

"Battle of Hastings Facts for Kids." *Kiddle Encyclopedia*. September 20, 2022. https://kids.kiddle.co/Battle_of_Hastings

"Bayeux Tapestry Facts for Kids." *Kiddle Encyclopedia*. July 5, 2022. https://kids.kiddle.co/Bayeux_Tapestry

"Beowulf Facts for Kids." *Kiddle Encyclopedia*. June 29, 2022. https://kids.kiddle.co/Beowulf

Britannica, T. Editors of Encyclopedia. "Anglo-Saxon." *Encyclopedia Britannica*. May 9, 2022. https://www.britannica.com/topic/Anglo-Saxon

Britannica, T. Editors of Encyclopedia. "Anglo-Saxon art." *Encyclopedia Britannica*. February 27, 2018. https://www.britannica.com/art/Anglo-Saxon-art

Britannica, T. Editors of Encyclopedia. "Norman." *Encyclopedia Britannica*. September 4, 2015. https://www.britannica.com/topic/Norman-people

Britannica, T. Editors of Encyclopedia. "Northumbria." *Encyclopedia Britannica*. August 20, 2013.

https://www.britannica.com/place/Northumbria

Britannica, T. Editors of Encyclopedia. "Wessex." *Encyclopedia Britannica*, May 5, 2020. https://www.britannica.com/place/Wessex-historical-kingdom

"Cantware (Kent)." *The History Files*. Kessler Associates. Accessed October 2022. https://www.historyfiles.co.uk/KingListsBritain/EnglandKent.htm

Castelow, Ellen. "The Battle of Hastings." *Historic UK*. Historic UK Ltd. Company. Accessed October 2022. https://www.historic-uk.com/HistoryMagazine/DestinationsUK/The-Battle-of-Hastings/

"East Engle (East Angles / East Anglia)." *The History Files*. Kessler Associates. Accessed October 2022. https://www.historyfiles.co.uk/KingListsBritain/EnglandEastAnglia.htm

"East Seaxe (East Saxons / Essex)." *The History Files*. Kessler Associates. Accessed October 2022. https://www.historyfiles.co.uk/KingListsBritain/EnglandEssex.htm

"Egbert 827-839." *Englishmonarchs.uk*. Accessed October 2022. https://www.englishmonarchs.co.uk/saxon.htm

"Egbert of Wessex Facts for Kids." *Kiddle Encyclopedia*. July 20, 2022. https://kids.kiddle.co/Egbert_of_Wessex

Harrison, Julian. "Who Were the Anglo-Saxons?" *British Library*. British Library Board. Accessed September 2022. https://www.bl.uk/anglo-saxons/articles/who-were-the-anglo-saxons#:~:text=The%20Anglo%2DSaxons%20were%20migrants,the%20fifth%20and%20sixth%20centuries

"History of Anglo-Saxon England Facts for Kids." *Kiddle Encyclopedia*. July 22, 2022. https://kids.kiddle.co/History_of_Anglo-Saxon_England

"How was Anglo-Saxon Britain Ruled?" *Bitesize*. BBC. Accessed October 2022. https://www.bbc.co.uk/bitesize/topics/zxsbcdm/articles/zqrc9j6#:~:text=Each%20group%20of%20Anglo%2DSaxon,power%20on%20to%20their%20children

Hudson, Alison. "Religion in the Anglo-Saxon Kingdoms." *British Library*. British Library Board. Accessed October 2022. https://www.bl.uk/anglo-saxons/articles/religion-in-anglo-saxon-kingdoms#:~:text=From%20the%20end%20of%20the,impact%20on%20Angl o%2DSaxon%20England

Jackson, Dr. Eleanor. "Later Anglo-Saxon Art." *British Library*. British Library Board. Accessed October 2022. https://www.bl.uk/anglo-saxons/articles/later-anglo-saxon-art

Johnson, Ben. "King Offa." *Historic UK*. Historic UK Ltd. Company. Accessed October 2022. https://www.historic-uk.com/HistoryUK/HistoryofEngland/King-Offa/

Johnson, Ben. "The Norman Conquest." *Historic UK*. Historic UK Ltd. Company. Accessed October 2022. https://www.historic-uk.com/HistoryUK/HistoryofEngland/The-Norman-Conquest

Johnson, Ben. "The Venerable Bede." *Historic UK*. Historic UK Ltd. Company. May 22, 2017. https://www.historic-uk.com/HistoryUK/HistoryofEngland/The-Venerable-Bede/

"Kingdom of Sussex Facts for Kids." *Kiddle Encyclopedia*. August 18, 2022. https://kids.kiddle.co/Kingdom_of_Sussex

Lambert, Tim. "Society in Anglo-Saxon England." *Local Histories*. 2022. https://localhistories.org/life-in-anglo-saxon-england/

Mark, Joshua J. "King Egbert of Wessex." *World History Encyclopedia*. UNESCO Archives. November 19, 2018. https://www.worldhistory.org/King_Egbert_of_Wessex/

Mark, Joshua J. "Kingdom of Mercia." *World History Encyclopedia.* UNESCO Archives. November 30, 2018. https://www.worldhistory.org/Kingdom_of_Mercia/

"Middle Ages: Alfred the Great." *Ducksters*. Technological Solutions, Inc. Accessed October 2022. https://www.ducksters.com/history/middle_ages/alfred_the_great.php

"Middle Ages: Norman Conquest." *Ducksters*. Technological Solutions, Inc. Accessed October 2022. https://www.ducksters.com/history/middle_ages/norman_conquest.php

"Middle Ages for Kids: Anglo-Saxons of England." *Ducksters*. Technological Solutions, Inc. Accessed September 2022. www.ducksters.com/history/middle_ages/anglo_saxons.php

Mingren, Wu. "How Anglo-Saxon England Made the Radical Change to

Christianity." *Ancient Origins*. Stella Novus. December 2019. https://www.ancient-origins.net/human-origins-religions/christianization-anglo-saxon-england-0013002

"Offa." *British Library*. British Library Board. Accessed October 2022. https://www.bl.uk/people/offa

"Offa of Mercia Facts for Kids." *Kiddle Encyclopedia*. September 23, 2022. https://kids.kiddle.co/Offa_of_Mercia

"The Anglo-Saxon Kingdoms: A Brief Guide for Kids." *Imagining History*. April 28, 2020. https://www.imagininghistory.co.uk/post/a-brief-guide-to-anglo-saxon-kingdoms

"The Canterbury Tales Facts for Kids." *Kiddle Encyclopedia*. April 9, 2022. https://kids.kiddle.co/The_Canterbury_Tales

"The Venerable Bede (673 AD - 735 AD)." *British Broadcast Corporation*. 2014. https://www.bbc.co.uk/history/historic_figures/bede_st.shtml

"What was Life like in Anglo-Saxon England?" *Bitesize*. BBC. Accessed October 2022. https://www.bbc.co.uk/bitesize/topics/zp6xsbk/articles/zphysk7#zx6sp4j10

Wood, Michael. "10 Ways the Anglo-Saxons Changed the Course of British History." *History Extra*. Immediate Media Company Limited. November 22, 2019. https://www.historyextra.com/period/anglo-saxon/michael-wood-how-what-did-anglo-saxons-do-british-history/